UNITED
WE STAND

Because you are but a young man, beware of temptations and snares; and above all, be careful to keep yourself in the use of means; resort to good company; and howbeit you be nicknamed a Puritan, and mocked, yet care not for that, but rejoice and be glad, that they who are scorned and scoffed by this godless and vain world, and nicknamed Puritans, would admit you to their society; for I must tell you, when I am at this point as you see me, I get no comfort to my soul by any second means under heaven but from those who are nicknamed Puritans. They are the men that can give a word of comfort to a wearied soul in due season, and that I have found by experience . . .

THE LAST AND HEAVENLY SPEECHES, AND
GLORIOUS DEPARTURE, OF JOHN, VISCOUNT KENMURE

UNITED
WE STAND

Thomas Brooks

Taken from
'Precious Remedies against Satan's Devices',
The Works of Thomas Brooks, Vol. 1

THE BANNER OF TRUTH TRUST

THE BANNER OF TRUTH TRUST
3 Murrayfield Road, Edinburgh EH12 6EL, UK
P.O. Box 621, Carlisle, PA 17013, USA

*

© The Banner of Truth Trust 2009

ISBN: 978 1 84871 028 3

*

Typeset in 10.5 / 13.5 pt Adobe Caslon Pro
at the Banner of Truth Trust, Edinburgh

Printed in the USA by
Versa Press, Inc.,
East Peoria, IL

*

Minor editorial adjustments have been made to the
original text, e.g. the modernizing of some words
and the supplying of Scripture references.

UNITED WE STAND, DIVIDED WE FALL

Satan has his devices to destroy the saints; and one great device that he has to destroy the saints is,

By working them first to be strange, and then to divide, and then to be bitter and jealous, and then 'to bite and devour one another' (Gal. 5:15).

Our own woeful experience is too great a proof of this. The Israelites in Egypt did not more vex one another than Christians in these days have done, which occasioned a deadly consumption to fall upon some.[1]

[1] If we knock, we break. Dissolution is the daughter of dissension.

REMEDY 1.

The first remedy against this device of Satan is,

To dwell more upon one another's graces than upon one another's weaknesses and infirmities.

It is sad to consider that saints should have many eyes to behold one another's infirmities, and not one eye to see each other's graces, that they should use spectacles to behold one another's weaknesses, rather than looking-glasses to behold one another's graces.[2]

[2] Flavius Vespasian, the emperor, was more ready to conceal the vices of his friends than their virtues. Can you think seriously of this, Christians, that a heathen should excel you, and not blush?

Erasmus tells of one who collected all the lame and defective verses in Homer's *Works,* but passed over all that was excellent. Ah! that this were not the practice of many that shall at last meet in heaven, that they were not careful and skilful to collect all the weaknesses of others, and to pass over all those things that are excellent in them. The Corinthians did eye more the incestuous person's sin than his sorrow, which was like to have drowned him in sorrow.

Tell me, saints, is it not a more sweet, comfortable, and delightful thing to look more upon one another's graces than upon one another's infirmities?

Tell me what pleasure, what delight, what comfort is there in looking upon the enemies, the wounds, the sores, the sickness, the diseases, the nakedness of our friends? Now sin, you know, is the soul's enemy, the soul's wound, the soul's sores, the soul's sickness, the soul's disease, the soul's nakedness; and ah! what a heart has that man that loves thus to look!

Grace is the choicest flower in all a Christian's garden; it is the richest jewel in all his crown; it is his princely robes; it is the top of royalty; and therefore must be the most pleasing, sweet, and delightful object for a gracious eye to be fixed upon.

Sin is darkness, grace is light; sin is hell, grace is heaven; and what madness is it to look more at darkness than at light, more at hell than at heaven![3]

Tell me, saints, does God not look more upon his people's graces than upon their weaknesses? Surely he does. He looks

[3] Not race or place, but grace truly sets forth a man.

more at David's and Asaph's upright-
ness than upon their infirmities, though
they were great and many. He eyes more
Job's patience than his passion; 'Remember the patience of Job', not a word of his
impatience (*James* 5:11).

He that drew Alexander whilst he had
a scar upon his face, drew him with his
finger upon the scar. God puts his fingers
upon his people's scars, that no blemish
may appear.

Ah! saints, that you would make it the
top of your glory in this, to be like your
heavenly Father! By so doing, much sin
would be prevented, the designs of wicked men frustrated, Satan outwitted, many
wounds healed, many sad hearts cheered,
and God more abundantly honoured.[4]

---

[4] Sin is Satan's work, grace is God's work; and is it not

REMEDY 2.

The second remedy against this device of Satan is, solemnly to consider,

That love and union makes most for your own safety and security.

We shall be invincible if we be inseparable. The world may frown upon you, and plot against you, but they cannot hurt you. Unity is the best bond of safety in every church and commonwealth.[5]

---

most meet that the child should eye most and mind most his father's work?

[5] There was a temple of Concord amongst the heathens; and shall it not be found among Christians, that are temples of the Holy Ghost?

And this did that Scythian king in Plutarch's book represent lively to his eighty sons, when, being ready to die, he commanded a bundle of arrows fast bound together to be given to his sons to break; they all tried to break them, but, being bound fast together, they could not; then he caused the band to be cut, and then they broke them with ease. He applied it thus:

My sons, so long as you keep together, you will be invincible; but if the band of union be broke betwixt you, you will easily be broken in pieces.[6]

Pliny writes of a stone in the island of Scyros, that if it be whole, though a large and heavy one, it swims above water, but

---

[6] Pancirollus said, that the most precious pearl among the Romans was called *unio*, union.

being broken, it sinks.[7] So long as saints keep whole, nothing shall sink them; but if they break, they are in danger of sinking and drowning.

[7] No doubt a volcanic, porous product.

Remedy 3.

The third remedy against this device of Satan is,

To dwell upon those commands of God that do require you to love one another.

Oh! when your hearts begin to rise against each other, charge the commands of God upon your hearts, and say to your souls, O our souls! has not the eternal God commanded you to love them that love the Lord? And is it not life to obey, and death to rebel?[8]

---

[8] To act, or run cross to God's express command, though under pretence of revelation from God, is as much as a man's life is worth, as you may see in that sad story (1 *Kings* 13: 24).

Therefore look that you fulfil the commands of the Lord, for his commands are not like those that are easily reversed; but they are like those of the Medes, that cannot be changed.

Oh! be much in pondering upon these commands of God.

A new commandment I give unto you, that ye love one another; as I have loved you, that ye also love one another (*John* 13:34).

It is called a new commandment, because it is renewed in the gospel, and set home by Christ's example, and because it is rare, choice, special, and remarkable above all others.[9]

---

[9] Some conceive it to be an Hebraism, in which language new, rare, and excellent, are synonyms.

This is my commandment. That ye love one another, as I have loved you . . .

These things I command you, that ye love one another. (*John* 15:12, 17).

Owe no man any thing, but love one another: for he that loveth another, has fulfilled the law (*Rom.* 13:8)

Let brotherly love continue (*Heb.* 13:1)

Love one another, for love is of God, and every one that loveth is born of God, and knoweth God (1 *John* 4:7)

See that ye love one another with a pure heart fervently . . . Finally, be ye all of one mind, having compassion one of another. Love as brethren, be pitiful, be courteous (1 *Pet.* 1:22; 3:8).

For this is the message that ye heard from the beginning, that we should love one another . . . And this is his commandment, that we should believe on the name of his Son Jesus Christ, and love one another, as he gave us commandment . . . Beloved, if God so loved us, we ought also to love one another. (1 *John* 3: 11, 23; 4:11).

Oh! dwell much upon these precious commands, that your love may be inflamed one to another.

In the primitive times, it was much taken notice of by the heathens, that in the depth of misery, when fathers and mothers forsook their children, Christians, otherwise strangers, stuck one to another, whose love of religion proved firmer than that of nature.

Ah! that there were more of that spirit among the saints in these days! The world was once destroyed with water for the heat of lusts, and it is thought it will be again destroyed with fire for the coldness of love.[10]

[10] The ancients used to say commonly, that Alexander and Hephaestion had but one soul in two distinct bodies, because their joy and sorrow, glory and disgrace, was mutual to them both.

REMEDY 4.

The fourth remedy against this device of Satan is,

To dwell more upon these choice and sweet things wherein you agree, than upon those things wherein you differ.

Ah! did you but thus, how would sinful heats be abated, and your love raised, and your spirits sweetened one to another! You agree in most, you differ but in a few; you agree in the greatest and weightiest, as concerning God, Christ, the Spirit, and the Scripture. You differ only in those points that have been long disputable amongst men of greatest piety and parts. You agree to own the Scripture, to hold to Christ the head, and to walk according to the law of the new creature.[11] Shall Herod and Pilate agree? Shall Turks and pagans agree? Shall bears and lions, tigers, and wolves, yea, shall a legion of devils, agree in one body? And shall not saints agree, who differ only in such things as have least of the heart of God in them, and that shall never hinder your meeting in heaven?

[11] What a sad thing was it that a heathen should say, No beasts are so mischievous to men as Christians are one to another.

REMEDY 5.

The fifth remedy against this device of Satan is, solemnly to consider,

That God delights to be styled Deus pacis, *the God of peace; and Christ to be styled* Princeps pacis, *the Prince of peace, and King of Salem, that is, King of peace; and the Spirit is a Spirit of peace. 'The fruit of the Spirit is love, joy, peace'* (Gal. 5:22).

Oh! why then should not the saints be children of peace? Certainly, men of self-willed, unquiet, fiery spirits cannot have that sweet evidence of their interest in the God of peace, and in the Prince of peace, and in the Spirit of peace, as those precious souls have that follow after the things that make for love and peace. The very name of peace is sweet and comfortable; the fruit and effect thereof pleasant and profitable, more to be desired than innumerable triumphs; it is a blessing that ushers in a multitude of other blessings[12] (2 *Cor.* 13:11; *Isa.* 9:6).

The ancients were inclined to paint peace in the form of a woman, with a horn of plenty in her hand.[13]

Ah! peace and love among the saints, is that which will secure them and their mercies at home; yea, it will multiply their mercies; it will engage the God of mercy to crown them with the choicest mercies; and

[12] Where peace is, there is Christ, because Christ is peace.

[13] The Grecians had the statue of Peace, with Pluto, the god of riches, in her arms.

it is that that will render them most terrible, invincible, and successful abroad. Love and peace among the saints is that which puts the counsels of their enemies to a stand, and renders all their enterprises abortive; it is that which most weakens their hands, wounds their hopes, and kills their hearts.

REMEDY 6.

The sixth remedy against this device of Satan is,

To make more care and conscience of keeping up your peace with God.

Ah! Christians, I am afraid that your remissness herein is that which has occasioned much of that sourness, bitterness, and divisions that be among you.[14] Ah! you have not, as you should, kept up your peace with God, and therefore it is that you do so dreadfully break the peace among yourselves. The Lord has promised that:

---

[14] There is no fear of knowing too much, but there is much fear in practising too little.

When a man's ways please him, he will make his enemies to be at peace with him (*Prov.* 16:7).

Ah! how much more then would God make the children of peace to keep the peace among themselves, if their ways do but please him!

All creatures are at his beck and check. Laban followed Jacob with one troop. Esau met him with another, both with hostile intentions; but Jacob's ways pleasing the Lord, God by his mighty power so works that Laban leaves him with a kiss, and Esau met him with a kiss; he has an oath of one, tears of the other, peace with both.

If we make it our business to keep up our league with God, God will make it his work and his glory to maintain our peace with men; but if men make light of keeping up their peace with God, it is just with God to leave them to a spirit of pride, envy, passion, contention, division, and confusion, to leave them 'to bite and devour one another, till they be consumed one of another.'[15]

---

[15] Phamaces sent a crown to Caesar at the same time he rebelled against him; but he returned the crown and this message back, *Faceret imperata prius:* Let him return to his obedience first. There is no sound peace to be had with God or man, but in a way of obedience.

REMEDY 7.

The seventh remedy against this device of Satan is,

To dwell much upon that near relation and union that is between you.

This consideration had a sweet influence upon Abram's heart:

And Abram said unto Lot, Let there be no strife, I pray thee, between me and thee, and between my herdsmen and thy herdsmen; for we are brethren (*Gen. 13:8*).[16]

---

[16] The Hebrew signifies, Oh! let there be no bitterness between us, for we are brethren.

That is a sweet word in the psalmist,

'Behold, how good and how pleasant it
is for brethren to live together in unity.
(*Psa.* 133:1)

It is not *good and not pleasant,* or *pleasant
and not good,* but *good and pleasant.* There are
some things that are good and not pleasant, as patience and discipline; and there are
some things that are pleasant but not good,
as carnal pleasures, and voluptuousness. And
there are some things that are neither good
nor pleasant, as malice, envy, and worldly
sorrow; and there are some things that are
both good and pleasant, as piety, charity,
peace, and union among brethren; and oh!
that we could see more of this among those
that shall one day meet in their Father's
kingdom and never part. And as they are
brethren, so they are all fellow-members:

Now ye are the body of Christ, and members in particular (1 *Cor.* 12:27).

And again:

We are members of his body, of his flesh, and of his bones (*Eph.* 5:30).

Shall the members of the natural body be serviceable and useful to one another, and shall the members of this spiritual body cut and destroy one another? Is it against the law of nature for the natural members to cut and slash one another?[17] And is it not much more against the law of nature and of grace for the members of Christ's glorious body to do so?

And as you are all fellow-members, so you are fellow-soldiers under the same

[17] The parti-coloured coats were characters of the king's children: so is following after peace now.

Captain of salvation, the Lord Jesus, fighting against the world, the flesh, and the devil.

And as you are all fellow-soldiers, so you are all fellow-sufferers under the same enemies, the devil and the world.

And as you are all fellow-sufferers, so are you fellow-travellers towards the land of Canaan, 'the new Jerusalem that is above'.

Here we have no abiding city, but we look for one to come.

The heirs of heaven are strangers on earth. And as you are all fellow-travellers, so are you all fellow-heirs of the same crown and inheritance.[18]

---

[18] *Rev.* 12:7-8; *Heb.* 2:10; *Rev.* 2:10; *John* 15:19-20; *Heb.* 12:14; 13:14; *Rom.* 8:15-17.

REMEDY 8.

The eighth remedy against this device of Satan is,

To dwell upon the miseries of discord.

Dissolution is the daughter of dissension. Ah! how does the name of Christ, and the way of Christ, suffer by the discord of saints!

How are many that are entering upon the ways of God hindered and saddened, and the mouths of the wicked opened, and their hearts hardened against God and his ways, by the discord of his people!

Remember this, the disagreement of Christians is the devil's triumph; and what a sad thing is this, that Christians should give Satan cause to triumph![19] It was a notable saying of one,

> Take away strife, and call back peace, lest you lose a man, your friend; and the devil, an enemy, joy over you both.

[19] Our dissensions are one of the Jews' greatest stumbling-blocks. Can you think of it, and your hearts not bleed?

REMEDY 9.

The ninth remedy against this device of Satan is, seriously to consider,

That it is no disparagement to you to be first in seeking peace and reconcilement, but rather an honour to you, that you have begun to seek peace.

Abraham was the elder, and more worthy than Lot, both in respect of grace and nature also, for he was uncle to Lot, and yet he first seeks peace of his inferior, which God has recorded as his honour.[20]

---

[20] They shall both have the name and the note, the comfort and the credit, of being most like unto God, who first begin to pursue after peace.

Ah! how does the God of peace, by his Spirit and messengers, pursue after peace with poor creatures! God first makes offer of peace to us:

> Now then, we are ambassadors for Christ, as though God did beseech you by us: we pray you in Christ's stead, be ye reconciled to God (2 *Cor.* 5:20).

God's grace first kneels to us, and who can turn their backs upon such blessed and bleeding embracements, but souls in whom Satan, the god of this world, kings it? God is the party wronged, and yet he sues for peace with us at first:

> I said, Behold me, behold me, unto a nation that was not called by my name (*Isa.* 65:1).[21]

---

[21] 'Behold me! behold me!' It is geminated [doubled]

Ah! how the sweetness, the freeness, and the riches of his grace break forth and shine upon poor souls. When a man goes from the sun, yet the sunbeams follow him; so when we go from the Sun of righteousness, yet then the beams of his love and mercy follow us.

Christ first sent to Peter that had denied him, and the rest that had forsaken him:

'Go your ways, and tell his disciples and Peter, that he goeth before you into Galilee: there shall ye see him, as he said unto you' (*Mark* 16:7).

Ah! souls, it is not a base, low thing, but a God-like thing, though we are wronged by others, yet to be the first in seeking after

---

to show God's exceeding forwardness to show favour and mercy to them.

peace. Such actings will speak out much of God with a man's spirit.

Christians, it is not matter of liberty whether you will or you will not pursue after peace, but it is matter of duty that lies upon you; you are bound by express precept to follow after peace; and though it may seem to fly from you, yet you must pursue after it:

> Follow peace with all men, and holiness, without which no man shall see the Lord (*Heb.* 12:14).[22]

Peace and holiness are to be pursued after with the greatest eagerness that can be imagined. So the psalmist:

---

[22] The Greek signifies to follow after peace, as the persecutor does him whom he persecutes.

Depart from evil, and do good; seek peace and pursue it (*Psa.* 34:14).

The Hebrew word that is here rendered *seek,* signifies to seek earnestly, vehemently, affectionately, studiously, industriously.

'And pursue it.' That Hebrew word signifies earnestly to pursue, being a metaphor taken from the eagerness of wild beasts or ravenous fowls, which will run or fly both fast and far rather than be disappointed of their prey. So the apostle presses the same duty upon the Romans:

Let us follow after the things that make for peace, and things wherein may edify another (*Rom.* 14:19).

Ah! you self-willed, sour, dogged Christians, can you look upon these commands of God without tears and blushing?

I have read a remarkable story of Aristippus, though but a heathen, who went of his own accord to Æschines his enemy, and said, 'Shall we never be reconciled till we become a table-talk to all the country?' and when Æschines answered he would most gladly be at peace with him, 'Remember, then', said Aristippus, 'that though I were the elder and better man, yet I sought first for you.' 'You are indeed', said Æschines, 'a far better man than I, for I began the quarrel, but you the reconciliation.' My prayer shall be that this heathen may not rise in judgment against the flourishing professors of our times,

Who whet their tongue like a sword, and bend their bows to shoot their arrows, even bitter words (*Psa.* 64:3).

REMEDY 10.

The tenth remedy against this device of Satan is,

For saints to join together and walk together in the ways of grace and holiness so far as they do agree, making the word their only touchstone and judge of their actions.

That is sweet advice that the apostle gives:

I press toward the mark for the prize of the high calling of God in Christ Jesus (*Phil.* 3:14-16).

Let us therefore, as many as be perfect [comparatively or conceitedly[23] so] be thus minded. And if in anything ye be otherwise minded, God shall reveal even this unto you. Nevertheless, whereto we have already attained, let us walk by the same rule, let us mind the same thing.

Ah! Christians, God loses much, and you lose much, and Satan gains much by this, that you do not, that you will not, walk lovingly together so far as your ways lie together. It is your sin and shame that you do not, that you will not, pray together, and hear together, and confer together, and mourn together, because that in some far lesser things you are not agreed together. What folly and madness is it in those whose way of a hundred miles lies ninety-nine

[23] Those who have reason to conceive themselves 'perfect'.

together, yet will not walk so far together, because that they cannot go the other mile together; yet such is the folly and madness of many Christians in these days, who will not do many things they may do, because they cannot do everything they should do. I fear God will whip them into a better temper before he has done with them. He will break their bones, and pierce their hearts, but he will cure them of this malady.

And be sure you make the word the only touchstone and judge of all persons and actions:

To the law and to the testimony, if they speak not according to this word, it is because there is no light in them (*Isa.* 8:20).

It is best and safest to make that to be the judge of all men and things now that all shall be judged by in the latter day:

The word [says Christ] that I have spoken, the same shall judge him in the last day (*John* 12:48).

Make not your dim light, your notions, your fancies, your opinions, the judge of men's action, but still judge by rule, and plead, 'It is written.'

When a vain importunate soul cried out in contest with a holy man, 'Hear me, hear me', the holy man answered, 'Neither hear me, nor I you, but let us both hear the apostle.'

Constantine, in all the disputes before him with the Arians, would still call for the word of God as the only way, if not to convert, yet to stop their mouths.

Remedy 11.

The eleventh remedy against this device of Satan is,

To be much in self-judging: 'Judge yourselves, and you shall not be judged of the Lord' (1 *Cor.* 11:31).

Ah! were Christians' hearts more taken up in judging themselves and condemning themselves, they would not be so apt to judge and censure others, and to carry it sourly and bitterly towards others that differ from them.[24] There are no souls in the world that are so fearful to judge others as

---

[24] It is storied of Nero, himself being unchaste, he did think there was no man chaste.

those that do most judge themselves, nor
so careful to make a righteous judgment of
men or things as those that are most careful
to judge themselves.

There are none in the world that
tremble to think evil of others, to speak evil
of others, or to do evil to others, as those
that make it their business to judge themselves.

There are none that make such sweet
constructions and charitable interpretations
of men and things, as those that are best
and most in judging themselves.[25]

One request I have to you that are
much in judging others and little in judging
yourselves, to you that are so apt and prone
to judge harshly, falsely, and unrighteously,

[25] In the Olympic games, the wrestlers did not put their
crowns upon their own heads, but upon the heads of others. It is just so with souls that are good at self-judging.

and that is, that you will every morning
dwell a little upon these scriptures:

Judge not, that ye be not judged; for
with what judgment ye judge, ye shall
be judged; and with what measure ye
mete, it shall be measured to you again
(*Matt.* 7:1-2).

Judge not according to appearance, but
judge righteous judgment (*John* 7:24).

Let not him that eateth not judge him
that eateth, for God has received him.
Why dost thou judge thy brother? or why
dost thou set at nought thy brother?

We shall all stand before the judgment-
seat of Christ. Let us not judge one
another any more, but judge this rather,
that no man put a stumbling-block or

an occasion to fall in his brother's way (*Rom.* 14:3, 10, 13)

Judge nothing before the time, until the Lord come, who both will bring to light the hidden things of darkness, and will make manifest the counsels of the hearts, and then shall every man have praise of God' (1 *Cor.* 4:5).

Speak not evil one of another, brethren: he that speaketh evil of his brother, and judgeth his brother, speaketh evil of the law, and judgeth the law; but if thou judge the law, thou art not a doer of the law, but a judge. There is one lawgiver, who is able to save and to destroy (*James* 4:11-12).

Who art thou that judgest another man's servant? to his own master he standeth or falleth; yea, he shall be holden up, for God is able to make him stand' (*Rom.* 14:4).

One Delphidius accusing another before Julian about that which he could not prove, the party denying the fact, Delphidius answers, 'If it be sufficient to deny what is laid to one's charge, who shall be found guilty?' Julian answers, 'And if it be sufficient to be accused, who can be innocent?' You are wise, and know how to apply it.

REMEDY 12.

The twelfth remedy against this device of Satan is this, above all,

Labour to be clothed with humility.

Humility makes a man peaceable among brethren, fruitful in well-doing, cheerful in suffering, and constant in holy walking (1 *Pet.* 5:5).

Humility fits for the highest services we owe to Christ, and yet will not neglect the lowest service to the meanest saint (*John* 13:5).

Humility can feed upon the meanest dish, and yet it is maintained by the choicest delicacies, as God, Christ, and glory.

Humility will make a man bless him that curses him, and pray for those that persecute him. An humble heart is an habitation for God, a scholar for Christ, a companion of angels, a preserver of grace, and a fitter for glory.

Humility is the nurse of our graces, the preserver of our mercies, and the great promoter of holy duties.

Humility cannot find three things on this side heaven: it cannot find fullness in the creature, nor sweetness in sin, nor life in an ordinance without Christ.

An humble soul always finds three things on this side heaven: the soul to be empty, Christ to be full, and every mercy and duty to be sweet wherein God is enjoyed.[26]

---

[26] Humility, said Bernard, is that which keeps all graces together.

Humility can weep over other men's weaknesses, and joy and rejoice over their graces.

Humility will make a man quiet and contented in the meanest condition, and it will preserve a man from envying other men's prosperous condition (1 *Thess.* 1:2-3).

Humility honours those that are strong in grace, and puts two hands under those that are weak in grace (*Eph.* 3:8).

Humility makes a man richer than other men, and it makes a man judge himself the poorest among men.

Humility will see much good abroad, when it can see but little at home.

Ah, Christian! though faith be the champion of grace, and love the nurse of grace, yet humility is the beautifier of grace; it casts a general glory upon all the graces in the soul.

Ah! did Christians more abound in humility, they would be less bitter, self-willed, and sour, and they would be more gentle, meek, and sweet in their spirits and practices.

Humility will make a man have high thoughts of others and low thoughts of a man's self; it will make a man see much glory and excellency in others, and much baseness and sinfulness in a man's self; it will make a man see others rich, and himself poor; others strong, and himself weak; others wise, and himself foolish.[27]

Humility will make a man excellent at covering others' infirmities, and at record-

[27] The humble soul is like the violet, which grows low, hangs the head downwards, and hides itself with its own leaves; and were it not that the fragrant smell of his many virtues discovered him to the world, he would choose to live and die in his self-contenting secrecy.

ing their gracious services, and at delighting in their graces; it makes a man joy in every light that outshines his own, and every wind that blows others good.

Humility is better at believing than it is at questioning other men's happiness. I judge, says an humble soul, it is well with these Christians now, but it will be far better with them hereafter. They are now upon the borders of the New Jerusalem, and it will be but as a day before they slide into Jerusalem.

An humble soul is more willing to say, Heaven is that man's, than mine; and Christ is that Christian's, than mine; and God is their God in covenant, than mine.

Ah! were Christians more humble, there would be less fire and more love among them than now is.

THE WORKS OF
THOMAS BROOKS

Thomas Brooks was born in 1608, probably of well-to-do parents. He entered Emmanuel College, Cambridge in 1625, following in the footsteps of such men as Thomas Hooker, John Cotton and Thomas Shepard. He was licensed as a preacher of the gospel by 1640. Before that date, he seems to have spent a number of years at sea, probably as a chaplain with the fleet. 'I have been some years at sea', he tells us, 'and through grace I can say that I would not exchange my sea experiences for England's riches.' 'Troubles, trials, temptations, dangers and deaths' were all encountered during his time on board ship.

After the Civil War, Brooks became minister at Thomas Apostle's, London, and was sufficiently well known to be chosen to preach before the House of Commons on 26 December 1648. He also served at St Margaret's, Fish-street Hill, London. The following years were filled with both written and spoken ministry.

In 1662 he fell victim to the notorious Act of Uniformity, but he seems to have remained in his parish and preached as opportunity arose. He married for a second time in 1677 or 78, but died only two years later in 1680.

His reputation as a writer of treatises for the heart has never been clouded. His literary style is always lively. Like many of his contemporaries he drew his sermon illustrations from the Scriptures themselves, from everyday life, and from ancient class-ical literature and history. The amalgam is invariably interesting and edifying.

A. B. Grosart quotes Calamy as saying that Brooks was 'a very affecting preacher and useful to many'. To this sombre word of praise he adds his own weighty verdict:

His slightest 'Epistle' is 'Bread of Life'; his most fugitive 'Sermon' a full cup of 'Living Water': . . . his one dominating aim to make dead hearts warm with the Life of the Gospel of Him who is Life; his supreme purpose to 'bring near' the very Truth of God. Hence his directness, his urgency, his yearning, his fervour, his fulness of Bible citation, his wistfulness, his intensity, his emotion . . . His desire to be 'useful' to souls, to achieve the holy success of serving Christ, to win a spark-ling crown to lay at His feet, breathes and burns from first to last.

OTHER BOOKS IN THE
POCKET PURITANS
SERIES

If you enjoyed reading this little book then you may be interested to know that the Banner of Truth Trust also publishes Thomas Brooks' *Precious Remedies Against Satan's Devices* (ISBN: 978 0 85151 002 6, 254 pp. paperback) in the Puritan Paperback series. The six-volume set of Brooks' *Works* (ISBN: 978 0 85151 302 7, approximately 600 pp. per volume, clothbound) is also published by the Trust.

For more details of these and all other Banner of Truth titles, please visit our website:

www.banneroftruth.co.uk

THE BANNER OF TRUTH TRUST

3 Murrayfield Road,
Edinburgh EH12 6EL
UK

P O Box 621, Carlisle,
Philadelphia 17013,
USA

www.banneroftruth.co.uk